C000135393

Poetry From the Heart:
Poems of Faith

Katherine B. Parilli

ISBN:
ISBN-13: 978-1-947238-00-8

De Graw Publishing
Okahumpka, Florida

DEDICATION

This book is dedicated to the memory of one of my greatest cheerleaders, my Grandfather, Edward Sepulveda. I know that he would have been proud of his little red head for chasing her dreams. How I miss our Sabbath afternoon chats and watching his face light up with pride when I succeeded in reaching one of my goals.

Poems of Faith

CONTENTS

Poems of Faith

ACKNOWLEDGMENTS

This book would not have been possible without the support of my parents They always believed in me and encouraged me to never give up on my dreams. Willingly sacrificing their time, money, and energy to help me reach my goals.

I would like to thank my little sister who like all younger siblings knew which buttons to press to irritate and annoy, but the very next moment inspired me with her belief that I could do anything.

Then there is my Grandmother who my sister and I lovingly refer to as "Mom." Sadly upon this earth the language barrier has prevented us from sitting down and holding a conversation without the aid of someone to interpret. But I would not have had the strength to make this book without the aid of her love and prayers. I cannot wait for Christ to come so we can finally sit down and I can tell her for myself how grateful I am for all of her prayers. Te quierro muchisimo Mom y gracias por tus oraciónes.

A special thanks to my Uncle John for all the times he fixed my computer. If it had not been for his computer savvy there are many times that I would have spent months without a working computer unable to get anything accomplished.

Also I would like to thank my Aunt Jeannette and Uncle Charles who dipped into their limited budget to pay for the professional photo shoot and the photograph that was chosen to be the author photo for this book. I really enjoyed the experience and I will always cherish the memory of that adventurous day.

And to my little pup Happy who curled up on my lap to see what I was doing and give his tail wag of approval.

But most of all I give thanks to God whose love has never failed me. I know that through trial and tribulation He has remained firmly by my side helping me to endure the hour of trial. Comforting me in my hour of need and lovingly revealing to me the short comings in my character.

I am convinced that His love knows no bounds. That is why He is the inspiration of every word that composes this book, but more importantly He is my hope and the source of my greatest joy.

Poems of Faith

Faith Gives us Courage to
Hang on No Matter the Storm

CHAPTER1
FAITH ACROSTICS 1-4

Acrostic 1

Faith
An act of
Inspiration and of
Total trust in
His holy care

Acrostic 2

Faith
An act of
intense devotion
To
His merciful watch care

Acrostic 3

Faith
An
intensive attempt
To walk with
Him who lifts us up from this world of sin

Acrostic 4

Faith
A total
Instinctive
Trust in the only One who can
Hold us above the deadly trapping tar pits waiting
to crush us under

A Season of Prayer and Reflection

CHAPTER 2
POETRY OF PRAYER

Dear Lord Help Me Today for I Seem to Have Lost My Way

Oh dear Lord please help me today for I cannot see my way.
The path I must follow seems to be buried in a fog of confusion.
My bearings are covered in a thick foam of anxiety and uncertainty.
My progression is painfully slow,
And I seem to have lost my way.

I want to move forward in faith,
But I have lost sight of the light that You sent to guide my way.
Surrounded by darkness I stumble upon the sharp piercing stones of doubt and distrust.
All the familiar guides are lost from my sight as I struggle to crawl my way through the dark cloud of self-trust that has blocked my view of Your light.

Oh dear Lord how I seem to be floundering in a sea of despair.
Floating in waves of crushing burdens and fear that block out the sky.
Tossing me helplessly from one shore to the next.
Just when I feel that I have found the right path another wave comes crashing and pulling me off to strange far away shores.

Help me today,
I plead with all the power a sin filled heart can muster,
To turn away from the paths of death.
To push away the dark clouds of self-trust and give every corner of my heart and life to You.
To wait patiently for Your faithful hand to light my way.
Instead of rushing ahead,
Insisting that I know my own way,
Let me follow humbly,
Guided by Your almighty wisdom.
Secured in Your protecting arms from which the

enemy cannot wrest.

Dear Lord please help me today.
Take away the pride of my sin filled heart.
Help me to despise the call of evil,
Of self-confidence,
And earthly desires that lead me astray.
Today I am lost in a world of cruel evil given over to
pride.
Unwilling to follow the gentle tug of the bridle,
But help me I pray to see and admit the errors of my
ways.
Asking humbly for forgiveness,
Giving You total control of my sin soaked heart.
Letting You lead me safely every step of life's way.

Never more to lose sight of Your faithful light that
illuminates my path.
Walking securely in the fountain of Truth that brings
freedom from the burden of sin,
Washing away my load of guilt in Your pure
undefiled blood.
Receiving that transplant that saves one from a life
time of love with sin.
Receiving a heart that prefers the ways of Heaven to
self-trust and lust for sin.

Oh grant me today,
I plead with all of the faulty faculties benumbed by
deadly sin,
I long with all the strength I can muster well dying in

sin,
Grant me a new heart.
Renew my stumbling faith.
Remove this curse of self-satisfaction,
A longing for earthly pleasure and riches.
Make me today a new person,
One that only You have power to create.
One who seeks the ways of peace,
Who longs for Heaven's grace.

Then at last the light of Heaven can illuminate the path.
Only when I have been fully emptied of self can this deep darkness be lifted.
For only then will I be willing to follow.
Willing to walk the lonely paths.
Ready to die for Thee,
Or be content to live the life of quiet patience.
Giving all the credit of success to The Creator who marked the way with His holy blood.
Waiting desperately to reach that final mile when at last my dust ridden earthly home pass away,
And at last I see my new Home eternal.

Dear Lord Please Make Me Useful for Thee

Dear Lord,

Savior of my foolish soul, transformer of my incessantly wicked heart, today I ask Thee, with the faintest dawning of Thy earth shaking power, remove forever the power of sin from my enslaved depraved human nature. And lift my darkly shrouded mind towards heaven's all piercing light.

Today, in honor of Thy pure redemptive power, undiluted by the decaying taint of sin. Reform my vile life, recreate in my putrid body the glorious symmetrical image of my Savior.

In this very hour, when I am so far from Heaven's holy gates, so unworthy of Thy unselfishly shed blood, make me anew. Make me a living monument of Thy redemptive sin consuming power. A little light house on a once sin dark hill pointing towards Heaven's sanctifying shore.

Oh dear Lord, accept this day this my feeble offering, bowed down with an inestimable weight of sin. A body bleeding and blistering with the sores of filthy lust and selfish desire is all I have to give. Yet a longing to be set free by Thy grace saving power has taken hold of my once world absorbed heart. Seeking to be a humble tool in the mighty master's hands I bow in humble contrition before Thy uplifted throne.

Hold me. Enfold me. Guide my once shipwrecked boat safely towards that glorious shore. And make it a memorial of Thy unending love.

Oh I pray, how I ask with longing questioning heart, that in some simple way, somehow, Thou use me to rescue other prisoners of the devil's wretched dungeon. That in the humblest manner, in the quiet of the evening, or in the early hours of the dawn my trembling hands held fast in the ones that formed the universe, be given strength to lift up Thy righteous name before the mocking throng.

In Thy holy Name I pray.
Blessing and honor be upon all Thy humble servants
Amen
Thy newest humble servant I pray

Dear Lord Please Come Quickly

Dear Lord, please come quickly. This world is a scary place to live. I am tired of the uncertainty of life and the building indifference to human life. The devil's furry at snatching souls grows stronger every day, and his hatred towards your helpless creatures is spreading through the human race. Wars and famine are not far from the headlines, but few people care. A new breed of evil is spreading through the world in the form of men who are so inspired by the devil with hate, that they walk the streets seeking innocent blood to shed with their own.

Children are no longer safe on the playgrounds from the bombs of the dissenter. The mother buying her day's bread must duck from the bullet of her neighbor, and the old lay dying from the cruel knives of the warring tribe. Feuds and wars are epidemic started for some mysterious reason.

Nature is growing weary of the abuse heaped upon her by heartless man. Groaning stronger and stronger with each abuse, and lashing her furry upon coast and mountain. Storms seem to be growing stronger and more frequent destroying what life and property war has yet to touch. From droughts to flood the days mesh together and uncertainty wearies the storm haggard mind.

My heart is growing tired of beholding death and sorrow. I wish the cries of the hungry and fearful could be forever silenced. And still as the storm rages on, human beings cling ever closer to evil. Their love of sin seems to grow with each merciful call to repentance.

Oh dear Lord you must be coming soon for I see the signs You mentioned in Your word. Acts of horror I never could have imagined greet me every day. And as the killer storm approaches shore, words of defiance pour forth from sin hardened lips. Laws to preserve life are being overturned as armies arise to greet a new enemy. The devil must be laughing merrily as he watches the world churning its way joyfully into destruction and calling out to God to undue the penalty of their evil course.

I am tired of sin and all its gore. My heart longs for the peace of Heaven. As a child grows weary watching the markers go by on a hot dusty trial, so my heart longs to see that last mile marker and catch a glimpse of Heaven's gate. There at last my weary soul will find rest, and sin will be no more. Hate and death, the enemy of God will at last be done away with. Only the cheerful voice of the child at play and the bird upon her nest will disturb my deep and curing slumber.

But at last Oh Lord, as much as my sinful heart complains for the gentle taste of punishment it so rightfully deserves, I must not forget the burden You bare for Your creation. As distraught as my sin scared soul is over the cruel hearts of man, how must the purity of Your perfect being reel from the reek of sin that greets You every hour. How Your heart must long for that final hour when You can declare the trial of sin over. And yet You bare long with us because You despise the thought of one sinner missing out on Heaven's last call.

What pain has Your pure heart endured on our behalf! What love that seeks so patiently for those who would call for Your destruction! My heart will never understand the depths of love that calls the killer to his knee and lifts them from the dungeon to the castle and turns his evil heart into one of love and purity. That you would deal so long with this sinful world and watch the once perfect creation take on the image of evil, must be worse than the nails that pierced Your hands at Calvary.

If I grow weary of sickness and death, how much harder must it be on the One who created us to know only love and everlasting life. No being suffering under a thousand tortures must long for the end of sin more. Our hunger for this world's food cannot match your desire to feed our hearts from the living word and quench our thirst from the River of Life. As the end of the war between good and evil draws to its climatic close, how deeply must You wish that it would not end with so few excepting your offer. If my evil heart desires an end to the drama of sin, how you must long to reach each sin stricken soul.

Thank you for your mercy and patience. I know you wait to come a little longer to reach just one more person. Perhaps you are waiting for me to heed the call and I do not even know that my fate still hangs in the balance. But out of love for earring sin stricken humanity you wait to plead one more time lest even one precious soul who might be saved is lost. My heart still longs for that great day when this rancid earth fades into distant memory, and I know that it will come sooner than I think, but thank you for waiting just a little longer to save a great sinner like me.

Father Forgive Me

Dear Heavenly Father,
Look down with patience upon thy humble,
Stumbling child.
Embroiled in sin,
Born under its devastating curse.

Have mercy upon this pitiful mortal form,
Battle scarred and weary,
Weighted down by the crushing penalty of
transgression.

Reach down and bless my uplifted hands,
And hear the groaning plea of my contrite heart.
No honor or glory can I plead,
No pocket of bountiful jewels can I bring,
Only bended knee and tear stained cheeks can I
offer.

Humbly lifting up my overwhelming need,
Relying upon Thy unsurpassed mercy,
I declare my sad record of sin with trembling lips.

Asking to be made pure,
To be washed whiter than snow,
And to stand innocent in Thy holy eyes.

Declaring my unworthiness,
I seek to be relieved from my heavy burden.
Excepting my guilt,
Acknowledge that I am worthy of death.
Trusting in Your saving arm,
I pour forth my greatest need,
Desiring a new heart more than riches,
And salvation more than earthly exaltation.

Oh Father in Heaven,
Hear my prayer,
Hear my plea.

When my name is called in the judgment,
See not my shameful record,
That ugly mountain of crushing guilt.

When my day of trial comes,
When my hour of rightful condemnation arrives,
Please see only Your Son.
Interpose His blood stained face between us.
Where I should rightfully stand,

Condemned and sentenced for rebellion,
Let His voice declare that my guild is no more.
That it has been purged by His sacrifice,
Buried in His atoning blood.
Oh please let Him pronounce before the eagerly
waiting worlds that He is my friend,
My brother,
My Savior.

May the Heaven's ring with triumphant shout that
He has purchased my life,
That He is my Redeemer.
With glad chorus repeating the wondrous news,
That this once confirmed sinner,
Is clean forevermore.
Has washed in the Life Giving Fountain,
And been reborn.

This my prayer,
My earnest petition,
Oh dearest Father and LORD of all,
That You would forgive and transform a deep seated
sinner like me.

BRING ME HOME TODAY
DEAR LORD

Bring me home today dear Lord. I am tired of living in this war torn world. The sound of the battle grows stronger all the time. The battlements of the enemy surround me. Every day they seek my soul.

Come soon for the army of the Devil grows bold. Their furry is strengthening, their hatred of your people is reaching the brim. Their wicked inspiration fills every corner of the earth.

I want to walk the peaceful streets. To rest beside still waters while I taste the luscious fruit of the Tree of Life while Angels pure and holy sing their most glorious songs. At last to rest in peace from the dreadful burden of sin. For eternity free from death!

For eternity free from fear! Safely in Thy borders will I dwell. Evermore secure from the deadly grasp of Satan's fiendish grip.

Come soon dear Lord and save my sin tainted soul. Remove the ugly film of sin and mold my heart into Thy pure image. Make me a new, and fill me with Thy spirit.

Come soon and fill this plagued world with Thy merciful justice. Come soon and show the scoffing world that You live! Come soon and put an end to the curse of misery and death. Forever more wipe away the Devil's blight.

Create me anew. Create the earth once more in its Eden glory. Come soon before this vile world shall self-destruct in the rickety boat of Satanic lust.

Seek God With all of Your Heart
and You Shall Find Him

CHAPTER 3
POEMS OF HEART
SEARCHING

HOW UNWORTHY AM I

How unworthy am I of your mercy.
I do not begin to deserve it.
There is nothing inside of me worthwhile to save.

Why God cares and died for me is a mystery.

It obviously is not for gain.
For there is no way I can ever repay him.

I am not rich.
I am not special.
I do nothing important.
Have not the knowledge of the world.
Nor the genius of a scientist.

What did Jesus hope to gain by dying for me.
It was not for gold.
Nor for raving beauty.
Definitely not for a genius.
And sadly not for a person who lives without sin.

Why would He give up His life for mine?
The deed makes no sense.
What could He have possibly seen in me?
Why did He take a chance on thankless me?

I never threw Him a party for His courage,
Or gave Him a medal of heroism.
I did not announce His deed to the media.
Write a story of His selflessness for the front page.
Tell His story to the breathless nation.
Nor ever gave a simple word of thanks.

Instead, I added weight to His burden.
I turned my eyes from His precious gift.
Closed my ears to His dying plea.
Helped to hammer the nails with my complete

indifference.

So why did He do it?
Why did He leave Heaven's glory to pay my price?
Turn His back on Angel's praises.
Drown out the adoration of hundreds of worlds.
Leave the holiest spot next to the Father of the Universe.
Come down to dreary earth.
Be born a poor baby.
Become the ransom of a sin-infested world.

The answer can be found in one place.
His heart.
A heart of love which is bigger than life itself.
Like the bond between a parent and their child.
Who willingly gives up all to help their helpless babe.
No gift or sacrifice too great for them to make.

No bond on earth can better describe it.
The tender love He held.
Making Him willing to be held ransom.
Risking all to die for a hopeless race.
Never asking a word of thanks.
Realizing there was no way to ever repay the debt.

I owe Him so much.
He looked past the grubbiness.
Saw through the exterior of uselessness.
Blinked at the ugliness.

He saw not what I was,
But what I could become.
Knew what I would become.
Knew that with His help I could be something good.
Leave behind the life of sin in His strength.

For seeing that through His death, my life would change.
My life would be the better.
He choose my salvation over His life.
My life was held so dear.
And oh, how unworthy of the gift I am!
Nothing I can ever do or say can ever hope to compare to His wondrous gift.
A gift of life, purity, happiness, and Heaven
Given to a worthless sinner such as me!

Where is My Faith

Where is my faith,
My unwavering trust in Thee?
Where is the power and endurance of my first love for You?
Where is that burning passion that cannot bear to see Your blessed name be besmirched so cruelly by the mocking throng?

All my life You have stood faithfully by my faulty side.
All my life You have been a ladder lifting me higher,
A crutch when my feet did fumble and fall,
And a guiding light when I was lost.

Through every trial You stood unflinchingly by my side.
When the masses gathered together to feast upon

my bruised an bleeding body,
You stood as a shield before my torn and tattered form.
As the insults poured forth like rain,
When left to blister under the scorching sun,
And the riotous scavengers gathered in cawing flocks to pick and devour the last dying vestiges of my soiled reputation,
You stood firm like a wall of blessing between me and my triumphantly taunting enemies.

Every bruise,
Every brackish bleeding wound that pierced my weak wounded soul,
You counted not as done to my worthless body,
But as done to Your precious Royal Holy Son.

Life and light were in Your wings.
In Your presence I found courage to face every storm.
Hope, love, safety, and peace were Yours to give.

Yet I faltered.
I have failed of climbing high.
Let the taunts of unclean hearts wear me down.
I have given my ear to foolish, fading promises.
Oh fill my heart once more.
Return me to my first love.
Never more to part from Thee!
Filled by Thy soothing refreshing spirit,
Undaunted by the sin maddened throng.

Let me put away my sin filled ways.
Despise the foolish paths I once loved.
Oh let me sing only of Thy righteous mercies,
Oh let Thy tender blessings be my abiding constant focus!

For You love,
For the lifting up of Your name,
Let my heart ever stand firm.
Hour after hour let me grow firm.
Closer and closer to Thy perfect ways,
Developing a symmetrical new beauty under the skillful potter's hand,
Let my heart entwine so close to Thee that I become like a newly grafted branch or vine that feeds fully and finds all its needs must naturally be satisfied by Thee.

Oh where is my first love?
Where is that deepness of power I should possess?
Where is that faith that will not yield even unto death?
Where is the fruits I should have born as the Sprit reformed my soul?

Make me anew!
Make me pure!
Fill me with Thy love!

Fill me full to overflowing before the door of mercy

closes.
Make me a light to the weary and despised.
Born again in the spirit,
And cleansed by Thy pure undefiled blood.

Today and forever let me be a part of Thy flock.
Willing to follow to the end.
Content to walk in the humblest ways.
Serving the servants of my king.

Oh bring back my love
Cleanse my heart today.
And fill me forever more with Thy purest gift of
love!

My Search for Peace

Earnestly I sought for joy.
In vain I combed every desert,
Climbed every mountain,
And swam every stream
Searching for inner peace,
Desperately seeking my purpose true.

Like a broken compass
Twirling in the breeze
I uselessly spun around
Seeking the balm of my heart.

Riches and poverty,
Fullness or hunger,
Could not fill the empty corner of my heart,
And could not pacify the deep longings of my soul.

Immersing myself in music,

Burying myself in work,
Drowning myself in pleasure
Could not silence the voice of inner turmoil.

Though I flew to the moon,
Though I drilled down into the center of the earth,
Though I studied the innermost mysteries of my
soul,
I found no peace,
I knew no joy.

For peace is more than a state of mind,
Purpose is more than seeking wealth,
And joy cannot be brought.
All of these are gifts from God.
All of these begin and end in Him.
They flow from Him like refreshing pools,
Nourishing hearts,
And restoring restless minds.

Though I spent a fortune,
Though I determinedly searched for many years,
The answer was not mine to inspire,
It was not mine to discover.

When at last I placed down my shovel,
Laid down my burden of I,
When in hopeless frustration I fell to my knees,
You were there.
Picking up the pieces,
Lifting my gaze,

And pointing me towards life's greatest tomorrows.

Now my restless soul is still.
Now my joy is complete.
For my selfish song of,
I will prevail,
I will carry the day,
I will win the battle,
I will climb the mountain,
I will win the golden crown,
I will..
I will…
I will…
Is quiet.

And in its place I sing a new song.
I have learned the glorious strain,
Thou art my Shepherd.
Thou art my hope.
Thou art my resting place.
Thou alone art my Savior.

Now I no longer need to search for prosperity.
No longer do I need to fight to be number one.
No longer do I need to grapple with the meaning of
success.

I do not have to search distant caves,
To trod across ancient lands,
Hoping and praying,
That I will discover life's purpose,

That I will stumble upon the meaning of life.

Now I know,
Now I understand,
That You gave me life.
You fashioned my bones,
You gave me voice.
You created me to love,
To honor,
And to serve you.
To live a life of noble faith.

Now I understand,
Now I realize,
That this is my purpose,
This is my song,
This is life's great destiny,
That I should give glory to Thee,
That I should give my all to Thee.
And now my heart is free
For my soul has found the key to eternal peace.

Trusting in the Arms of Love

CHAPTER 4
POEMS OF TRUST

HE CARRIES ME THROUGH

Sadly, I spend another long night watching the
seconds tick by the living room clock.
Watching and waiting for the next hour to start.
Hoping that morning's light would find me lost in
peaceful slumber.
My pain racked body dreaming of the time when it
could relax without fear of more discomfort.

The endless hours blurring together.
There is nothing to distinguish one hour from the next.
Hour after hour is filled with endless pain.
The only change is the ever-growing need for rest.
My eyes wanting only to drop quietly to sleep.
To close for many hours and days to come.

Still, the pain goes on even though the clock has already struck well past one,
And my body cries out for the rest it has yet to receive,
What can I do?
There is nothing to relieve the endless burning felt inside of my chest.
My stomach has become a heavy rock laden chamber dried out by drought.
Leaving the rocks to rip against each other while lacerating the tender coating into useless pieces,
A heavy green coat has covered my once red tongue, keeping away all taste except its own.
Nothing in my body is working right,
And no one knows what to do.

Desperately I cry out for the help which no one can give.
Trying endless medicines and treatments.
Wishing at times that my sickness would flee or leave me to the quiet peace of death.
Many times, I felt that there was nothing to keep me going on.

Life no longer seemed worthwhile.
Everything was filled with pain and tiredness.
Only one thing kept me going,
and one thought was there to give me hope.
That thought was of You.
And to the promises You gave.
They were my bread.
The icing upon which I could feast.
When all else failed they brought me comfort.
On days when my stomach could not be filled,
They gave me strength to continue on.
Your great love was my inspiration.
Carrying me above my plight for a precious moment.

Thank you God for all of your love.
Thank you Lord for filling my soul.
Thank you Savior for standing ever by my side.
You were there when I needed you.
Promising me all of Heaven to get me through my
pain.
Painting a picture of a brighter tomorrow.
Bringing my mind to other things.
Lifting my heart above earthly clouds.
Never complaining when I was weak,
But gently leading me on.

You changed my life.
Made my pain worthwhile.
For I knew when things were at their worst that was
when you stood the closest by my side.
Every night you stood there by my bedside.

Tonight, you are here again.
And I know tomorrow will find you here just the
same as before.
Until life's last breath is drawn,
I know that the Host of Heaven will peer over my
small place of restless tossing turning.
Most of all, and best of all,
I know that the King of all Creation is by my humble
side.
Patiently caring for my simple needs,
Gently rocking me to sleep,
Listening to my incoherent prattles with a
sympathetic ear,
And ever lifting my weary head to show me a
brighter tomorrow.

I Trust and Wait

I sit and wait.
Wondering
Praying
Working
Hoping

Dreaming of what may be,
I ponder,
Imagine,
Envision.

Knowing that the best is yet to be,
I struggle,
Persist
And pursue.

Ever trusting in Him who holds the future
I watch,
I wait,
I hope,
And stubbornly cling to His mighty hand.

I Will Trust in My Lord

I will rejoice in the great power and unmatchable mercy of my Lord forever. My heart will be humbled by the story of His great sacrifice to save mankind. In the heat of the storm, when the world looks like it will crumble around my feet, I will seek shelter in his all-encompassing arms, and find comfort in His holy word.

For He has granted me a second chance at life. In times of trial He has carried me through and grasped my weak and trembling hands in His. I have never known a pain or felt the pangs of hunger that He has not stood by my side pointing me upward. Gently has He reproved my faltering selfish ways and lovingly reminded me that He sacrificed all to save my soul. When refining my soul in the fire of trial, He held me close to lessen the pain. I have never known a time that He has left my side. He has shared my tears, endured the insults sent my way, and searched for me when I have wandered from His side.

In the arms of God there is a security no man can steal, no thief can understand. Though the world falls apart around me, His hand will lead me safely through. And if by chance He should let me sleep, His faithful eye will mark the sight. Though mountains fall, oceans dry, and fire melt the earth, His power to keep man's soul will not be broken. The devil may scream, the world's armies encamp about, but their arrows cannot pierce the heart whose armor comes from God.

Someday this world of sin will pass away. Its time of trial is almost over. The storm clouds of the final battle loom ever closer, and the devil's anger is growing stronger. Yet peace will I find in His shadow. He will hide me from the storm. For a little while the world will know His anger, for a time they will see His righteous anger towards sin. Still He will not forget his people. They will not be left to endure the trial alone. And from the Red Sea he will bring them safely over to the Promised Land.

There in the unfading beauty of Heaven they will forget the trial that brought their souls low. Safely sitting under the cooling branches of the Tree of Life, they will forget the intense sorrow of yesterday, and never again know fear. There they will walk the golden streets and talk of the great mercy of the One who brought them through that little storm. As the lame jump like the deer, the blind behold the endless beauty of the grassy hill, and the mute sing with the angels' choir, they will forget how cruel and barren life had seemed. The memories of the deaf will be replaced with the sounds of chattering birds, the purr of lions, and frolicking streams. The cries of the hungry will be heard no more as they feast at the wedding banquet, the poor will cast off their earthly rags and dine as equals of kings and queens. The freshness of youth will never fade, and there will always be new adventures to bring delight. The scientist will marvel in the wonders of creation, while the child plays with the leopard.

As I face the devils intense storm, my soul will find its strength in Heaven's delight. My heart's longing will be placed in the land where sin cannot spoil and the tempter destroy. Lost I pray will be the hold of this earth's fleeting vanity. May in that darkest hour, I remember that all the wealth and glory this world has to offer will melt in the heat of God' s quenching fire where sin is forever destroyed. From its smoky ashes will be built a new land where death and want will never be known. Free from the scares of sin I can run like the wind, sing the sweetest song, and my heart will be free from the heavy burden of sin.

Oh Dear Lord I pray that I will place my trust solely in You. That even if the world cast me away and my home is found in the dark and dreary caverns, that my heart will remain steadfast and secure in Your fortress where the devil cannot reach. Let me glory only in Your mercy, find praise in Your holiness, and security in Your perfection. May my sins be washed away in that undefiled blood and my heart created anew in Your undimmed image. May this ever be my prayer and the hope of my sin weary soul.

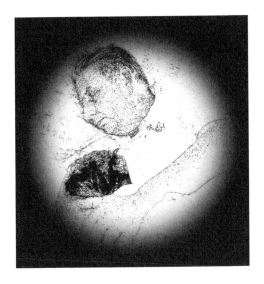

I Will Trust You

I will trust you because you will lead me besides the
still and safe quiet waters though the mountains
should fall and the trumpets of war blast.
I will trust you because when I call you will hear my
trembling voice amidst the boiling, swirling, devil
inspired storm.
I will trust you because when I fall you will lift me
up from the lowest pit of human degradation,
From the vilest pit of devilish inspired satanic frenzy,
And lift me up to the grandest pinnacle of heavenly
beauty and inspiration;
Creating a new creature with new lofty dreams,
A pure noble heart,
Recreated to reflect Thy noble beauty and grace of
character more and more each precious day.

I will trust you because when I am uncertain you point the way, like a compass sure and true you keep me safely and securely on the straight and narrow path.

I will trust in You because when I am alone, when all the world has turned and walked away, You are right there standing by my side like an unflinching wall of fire to keep out the arrows of Satan,

And yet at the same moment a gentle comforting arm to lean upon,

A cushioning shoulder to cry out ones tears,

A tender ear who will hear every whispered rung out woe,

An answering sympathetic heart that will feel each and every pain and bend low to comfort and secure each bruised and bleeding child,

And to lift up and support every confused and wondering soul.

I will trust in You because there is no other who has given so much and who has asked so little in return.

I will trust in You because you have given Your all at Calvary's cross to give me and the rest of this ungrateful world hope.

A second chance to walk with our heads held high knowing that even though we have no right,

That even though we do not deserve it,

God chose to step off His throne,

To take off His royal robes,

And purchase with His blood our chance at eternal happiness,

Our second chance at having eternal hope.

I will trust You because you love me with a love that
knows no bounds and cannot be expressed by the
highest of poetical praise.
I will trust You because for some unknown reason
You want me to spend all eternity with You in Your
kingdom,
And that love was so great that You gave Your life at
Calvary so that I could have that chance,
And what more could I do than to say yes Lord I
trust You with my life now and forever!

Surrender Your Heart to God
And Watch the Flowers of Change Bloom

CHAPTER 5
POEMS OF SURRENDER

May My Desire be Only for Thee

No matter the road.
No matter the cross.
Let my cry,
Let my plea,
Be only centered around,
Be only concentrated on,
Be only for Thee!

Only by Your Strength

I am endowed with no special gift.
Nothing great lies within.
There is no worthiness on my own.
Only with your assistance,
Only with your aid,
And only with your help can anything be done.
I must lean on you.
Surrender my will to yours.
For without you, my voice is useless.
The pen is a senseless tool.
The hand is only a helpless appendage.
You Lord are my strength,
My tower of encouragement,
A shield from the storm,
My comfort in sorrow,
And my tender friend even in trial.
To do Your will is joy.

You do not leave me to flounder on my own.
When I need You, You are right by my side.
Silently imparting strength to continue on.
Giving wisdom of what to do and say.
On my own nothing would be done.
No hungry soul could be feed.
No thirsty sheep watered from Thy eternal fountain.
The bread of life would mold,
Unusable in my unskilled hands.
Trusting in You gives me strength.
Leaning on Your arm gives me hope.
Giving my will to You allows a spring of blessing to flow.
Thank you for staying by my side.
For never leaving me to flounder helplessly,
Making me a part of your work.
All glory goes to You.
Only You deserve the praise of billions.
The worlds can worship Thee with joy.
For You give life and joy to all!

He Leads Me

He leads me,
But I know not where.
He guides me past a world of fears-
Lifting me up lest I fall.
Upon His bruised shoulders
He places life's heaviest burdens.
Carrying the bundles meant for me,
He leads the way through dark forest and down the
steepest trails.

In pathways forgotten and overgrown He cuts the
trail.
Each day He studies the path,
Marking the way with His precious blood-
Spilled freely on my behalf.
Whenever I falter He lifts me up,
Carrying me over rugged mountains,
And past deadly rocky cliffs.

45

Safely past the baying wolf,
Past the hungry lions,
Or the den of poisonous vipers,
He guides my trembling foot.
I need not fear the tigers maddening cry,
The shriek of celebrating hyenas,
Or the bone piercing teeth of the smiling crocs.

Past quicksand, around deadly pits, and avalanching
rocks
He agilely averts each new danger.
When the tempest blows with gnashing teeth,
He calmly blocks the deadly storm.
The mountains may crumple,
Waters rise to crushing heights,
And the earth may split beneath our feet,
Yet fearlessly He leads on.

The overwhelming forces of the Devil gather upon
the ridge to hem our way,
Yet with quiet dignity He raises His nail scared
hands-
Those nail pierced hands that bled for me-
And the soul frenzied forces of man hungry sharks
become as blind whimpering pups.
Discomfited by His pure powerful presence,
They scatter away helplessly in every direction
With their defeated tails tucked insecurely between
their slip sliding legs.

On we march in cold and heat.
Leading me to paths I would not chose on my own.
Paths filled with self-denial,
Made dark by human desire to seek an easier way.
Uncertainty fills my weary soul,
And oh how I long to find another way.
To be free of my burden-
Made light by the inhuman load He so willingly carries,
Made heavy by my selfish heart
That chooses to dwell so long upon my little burden,
Instead of honoring the man who took the heaviest load.

In weak and dangerous moment like those not a word of chastisement He speaks.
Just lifts the same nail scared hands that made the devils quakes.
With love flowing from those patient eyes He turns
And gazes silently into my selfish heart.
The love-
Unspeakable love I meet in those soul-searching eyes.
The memory of burdens He carried on my behalf,
The vision of the lonely cold cross He endued patiently,
Rise before my sin fainting heart.

I see the sacrifice He made for me.
I remember the agony He endured in my place.
When I think of the times He carried me safely

through the field of death,
Past swirling river,
Through mountains of frozen snow,
And through patches of thick mire,
How can I bare the sorrow I now behold upon His
sleepless worn face?

A face worn from guiding me through life's cruel
storms
Guarding me night and day from marauding pirates,
Wild beast,
Stannic frenzies.
Enduring privations on my behalf,
Marking the trail with His Holy blood and selfless
tears.
Quietly I gaze upon the scared hands,
Bearing the wounds rightfully meant for me.

For my sins He suffered abuse.
Endured the taunts of brutal man,
And was stripped and scourged to set me free from
the power and penalty of sin.
Oh how can I,
Ungrateful wretch turn and flee,
My burden so light as He alone pulls the load,
My way made straight,
As He clears the road.

On He leads once more I know not where.
Safely He guides me through the raging storms.
Traveling on to the home He built for me.

Leaving behind at each crossroad,
Another burden of selfish heart.
Fever buried by His blood soaked robes.
Exchanging my worthless spotted human nature
For a reflection of His spotless life.

Putting off my filthy rags to one day be clothed in
His royal robes.
One day to be called a child of the king.
Living not the life of one justly condemned as a
traitor of Heaven's righteous authority,
But to walk golden streets in that priceless land
where angel's live.
And cast of my earth worn shoes in exchange for the
palm branch of victory,
And a crown of glory this world cannot ever steal
from me.

Though today He leads me through paths loaded
with tedious care,
Though I know not where I shall rest my weary
head,
Or with what I shall fill my hungry belly,
I shall not flinch from the refiner's fiery hammer.
I shall not flee from the heavy blows
He must use to chip away the cracked and rotten
Rocks of sin infested fool's gold that stands between
me and Heaven's gates.

As He leads me through the Red Sea,
The stench of death

And calls to evil rising high on every side,
I can always pause to hear Heaven's impatient call
The song of angel's pleading for me-
Mingling their cries with His unceasing call to me.

Oh world where is your power when I hear that love
inspired choir?
Earth what is your attraction when He calls my
name?
Let Him lead me into paths unknown,
Through fire and storm-
Past roaring lions-
Ragging floods-
And foaming devils.

Though the world convulse in horror,
Though the sun doth fail,
Even if the buzzards gather above my weary head,
I shall cling to Him.
As He leads me through paths unknown,
Fraught with dangers,
Hemmed in by sorrow and despair,
I shall follow.

Where He leads me I will humbly go.
Safe from pride and conceit He shall keep me.
Leading me to still and quiet waters so delicate and
pure.
Soon to feast upon Heaven's sweet fruit,
Never more to roam path's unknown.

One day I shall behold those loving eyes.
Held close I in the arms that carried me through life's toughest trials.
Kept safe in the paths He chooses.
Marked by the blood He spilled so mercifully for me.
So one bright day He could carry me to Heaven's glorious abode.
There to live with Him eternally.

How I need thee

How I need Thy help to uncover the desires of my soul.
To lead me in the paths of righteousness,
To teach me how to thrive and grow,
To show me how to prosper,
And become an integral part of society.
Yet like a blind eagle
I vainly seek the exploding power of the thermals
So that I can soar to mighty heights unhampered by the dampening forces of earth.
But in my own power I am a useless,
Broken toy,
Rotting in some forgotten corner.
Waiting and begging for a chance to shine.

Lord I need Thy guidance.
I need Your help to unlock the unseen corners of my dusty heart,
and restore my creaking mind,
Make me over clean and fresh to reveal the purpose of my life.

I have no clue why or how,
But Thou,
The Maker of Clay and Life,
The Potter of Infinite Master Pieces
Does know my rightful use.
You created me to seek and to serve,
To think and to build,
To imagine and create,
To learn and to do,
To seek and to find,
To explore and to ponder,
And to sing and praise Thy holy name.

For seeking thy unending depths of wisdom,
For plunging thy unfathomable well of knowledge,
You built this frail body.
You endowed me with the skills
That I would need to endure each trial
And to Climb each daunting sky rising hill.
For your pleasant service I was formed,
And to fill this spinning earth with Your knowledge
I was born.

Today dear Lord,
I am lost,
I cannot find my way,
But onward I seek vainly to reach my uncertain goal.
My energies exhausted,
My hopes do fade.
My only hopes lies in Thee,
The Master of My wave tossed ship.

Tonight I go to Sleep

Tonight I go to sleep never more to wake.
Tonight I go to a rest from which no human can wake me-
To a repose from which nothing can disturb.

Do not shed your tears.
Save them for another less fortunate than me.
For I go to a rest that is good.
No more harm do I feel.
My pain is over.
The sleep is easy.

Do not fear my pain.
I am not scared.
I know what happens in this rest.
I am not really sad-
Though at times I shed a secret tear.
But my tears are not all for me.
They are for my friends with whom I once shared

children's dreams.
They are for those with whom I walked the path of
youth,
Speaking secret dreams that were growing,
Widening into unspeakable glory.

My tears are for my family.
The ones who always were beside me,
Caring for me when in need,
Holding my hand in pain,
Giving me all the love I need.

The tears I shed at one heart beat is for the family I
will never know.
The love I never will have.
Never to know the joy of the first date,
The thrill of that special question,
Or to know the honor of the wedding day.

I cry for the children I will never have.
The family I always wished to raise.
Growing old with that special someone.

But when I dry those selfish tears,
I realize that all is not lost.
True I lost these earthly memories,
And I never know these special moments,
Yet my rest is pure and sweet.
No one can wake me,
No hand can touch me.

And when I awake,
My eyes shall see Him in the sky.
Meeting my Savior.
Reuniting with all my friends.

What pain is death,
Where is its sting,
When all one does is sleep.
Resting until Jesus comes and calls;
Asleep in the safety of the dark depths of earth,
And then waking up to heaven's greatest glory.
Taking part in His second coming.

Never more to hurt.
Never more to feel pain.
Never more to sleep the sleep of death.

Joining the living I will rise.
Staring straight into my Jesus' eyes.
Never more to part.

You Cannot Learn to Love Someone
Unless You Spend Time With Them

CHAPTER 6
POEMS OF LOVE

Just Another Baby

Long ago in a barn hewn out of rocks a young mother gave birth. There was no doctor or scurrying nurses to attend to her. Only her husband, a carpenter by trade. When her little child was born, there was no soft and warm cradle to lay Him in only a manger full of hay.

To human eyes and hearts, it seemed to be the birth of another poor child in an already crowded world. Yet, unseen by any human eye, thousands upon thousands of angels waited breathlessly for this humble birth. Then all heaven rang with glorious songs of praise as the baby boy was gently laid in the pale mother's arms.

With the tender awe of every new mother, she counted His tiny toes and fingers. Quietly she whispered His name as she laid her precious bundle in a manger to sleep. As the young mother and her husband watched the precious infant sleep, angels kept careful guard. Their hearts filled with awesome wonder of their adored leader who willingly had lowered Himself. Who had left a perfect world, the beauty of never dying flowering meadows, majestic forest, choirs raised in perfect chords, and the glorious throne where He sat next to the Father as countless perfect beings worshiped Him with solemn joy.

That He would leave it all to come to a world laden with sin. A place so dark and dreary full of misery, hate, and death. That He would leave it all to become a lowly human baby, and grow into a man well accustomed with sorrow. Someday to hang on a cross for a race of people who had forfeited the right to life so they might have a way to live.

Love, praise, and adoration filled their hearts as they watched their sleeping King. A little baby sleeping peacefully in a smelly manger as the new parents looked on. Just another baby in an overcrowded world, or was He?

Love is the gift of greatest price

Love is the gift of greatest value,
Of greatest price.
For she causes one and all to bear great burdens.
There is not one,
Not even the bravest of soldiers,
Or the wisest of men
Who from her mighty power can hide.
Though they lock themselves behind mighty walls,
Cannot cloister themselves from every emotion,
Or hide from her mighty power,
And must at some point feel her fierce emotion.

Though one should try,
By hiding themselves in a lonely desert,
Or by wrapping themselves away in a dark tunnel,
They cannot shield themselves from every feeling,

action, and deed of love.

For love is like a precious flower,
Who must gently reveal each and every shivering
petal to the cruel cold world
If her sweet fragrance is to spill forth in precious
undimmed beauty.
Indeed, in the world of love there are only fragile,
trembling houses of glass,
Each seeking,
Each longing,
Each hoping,
That their next encounter will not be with a bat,
A stone,
Or a heartless cruel semi that will thoughtlessly ram
its way through their delicate walls.

All too often we do not understand,
Or appreciate love's peculiar or special blessing
As we ignore or berate that which we already have.
Maybe it is for those of us who do not yet have,
Who must still admire from afar to appreciate love's
special beauty.
To understand love's singular blessing upon the
heart and home.
To notice how it seems to lighten every load,
To lift every burden,
To bring cheer even to the loneliest of places.

For the man or woman who has found true love
And clings to it with all of their might is never truly

alone.

They are never alone,
Even when one is at work and the other is at home.
For their hearts are knit together,
And they know that nothing can break them
For they are tied by a promise made in front of the
everlasting throne of the Holy One,
For they have given their word to God.

Though they cannot not see Him,
They can feel His presence.
Though they cannot touch Him,
They can feel Him binding them closer and closer
together each and every day
With chords of mercy,
Uniting their hearts with heavenly affection made
strong by the softening power of the blood of the
lamb.

With love like that,
with earnest devotion on their part,
A great deal of daily prayer,
And spending time together to renew and strengthen
their relationship
How can they fail?

After all, when God is on your side,
When you cling to Him,
And remain faithful to Him
Where can you go wrong?

Love is a precious gift.
It is a special gift.
It is a gift straight from Heaven.
It fills the heart with wonder.
It overflows and fills the soul,
And then begins all over again.

Nothing Can Express the Depth of His Love

Words cannot express,
Voice cannot convey,
Song cannot impress,
Speech cannot inspire,
The greatness of His power,
The brilliance of His love.

A drop in the ocean,
We do not understand.
A grain of the Himalayas,
We have yet to comprehend.
So little is our appreciation of His goodness,
So incomplete is our estimation of His
righteousness.

For all eternity we shall study,

And yet have ages more to learn.
Though the pages of His sacrifice were worn away,
By constant study,
And our minds were to spend a billion years in solid
contemplation of His mercy,
Our eyes would still glow with wonder,
Our hearts still thrill with new delight.
As through the ceaseless ages,
Fine threads of His love weave the story of love,
To create an ever more perfect revelation of His
unselfish love before our grateful eyes.

The Lonely Cross

The unshed tears and heart of pain no one seems to
see or care.
On days of joy all joined the merry.
But now, when the heart is at its lowest, the tears of
sacrifice are at their peak, who cares or seems to
notice.
A heart full of love now hangs dying condemned of
men unseen.
Who stops to give a loving look, a word of comfort?
The weight of the world are upon those noble
shoulders.
When no more it seems that they can bear, upon
them are thrust words of jeer.
No hand to wipe the brow of its bloody sweat
caused by the weight of unjust sin.

The Father's love veiled from Him who will listen to

His cry or hearken to His plea.
Upon His brow the thistle tears His tender flesh the wound to bare.
Who will cover the wounded man when angels must veil, the sight for them too harsh to see.
The earth alone doth cover Him with a veil of darkness.
As if the sight of this lone man is too great a sight for any to see.
Who will help when all have turned who once sung His praises now drunk with His blood.
A voice cries from the darkness.
It is done!
It is done!
With a last cry His life is gone.
The earth trembles and then all is calm.
The gawking crowd leaves.
The last taunts given.

Expectations of Things Yet to Come

CHAPTER 7
POETRY OF EXPECTATION

Am I Ready to Meet the King?

Am I ready to meet the King of Glory?
Am I ready to join the angels in their song of praise?
Am I ready to shout for glory when the King comes through the gate?
Am I ready to waive the victory banner high and bid goodbye to this world?
Am I ready to victoriously march on those golden

streets?
Am I ready to eat the fruit of the Tree of Life?
Am I ready to live among those who never
wandered from the fold?
Am I ready to honor God with voice and life?
Am I ready to stand before a holy God when my
name is called?

How close to the Threshold of Heaven do I Stand?

How close am I to crossing over the border?
When will the cup of earth's iniquity be full?
And when will the door of mercy forever close?

I have grown weary of this world.
My eyes are tired of beholding sin.
My ears do throb from the shouts of vile rabble.
The cries of the widow ascend without ceasing.
And the fears of the oppressed weigh down upon

my soul.

When will the trumpet sound?
When will the shout of victory ring though out
eternity?
When will the power of the merciless be cut short?
Oh how long till the ugly day of sin come to its final
close?

The wicked gather in the streets to mock Thy
people.
They exult at the suffering poverty of their prey.
Pushing the poor from their shanty dwellings to
make room for their jewel decked mansions.
Demanding an ever-increasing wealth to feed theses
sharks of the land.
They hear not the father's pleas of mercy for his
children's empty bellies,
Or a mother's prayer for the protection of her sick
child.

How long till the heavens be rolled back?
How long till the sign of the Son of Man appear?
How long till the kingdom of the devil is destroyed?
How long till justice once more fills the land?

Works of wickedness grow bolder each day.
They have no thought of pity for young or old.
Their ears are stopped to the painful moans of the ill
or injured.
Their only thoughts are of evil and how to increase

their vicious power.

Should not that day be drawing near?
Is not that hour upon us?
Is not the host of Heaven gathering the last sheaves
before the harvest?
Is not this increasing of sorrows a sign of Your sure
return?
Are You drawing near the door?

The earth is growing weary.
Storms are brewing at every turn.
Pounding land and sea with frightful furry.
The earth rolls and rises as if convulsing.
Like a feverish patient it reels and stumbles
Mercilessly seeking comfort.
Spewing its troubled contents,
Waiting for its day of healing.

Yes the day must be near.
The hour must be drawing close.
For Thou art a God of justice.
Only mercy and love are hidden within Thy wings.
As a loving father seeks the good of his children,
Thou has waited patiently for our return.
Yet Thy justice demands an end to sin.
Thy mercy must vanquish the cruel foe,
 and bring an end to human suffering.

Soon,
So soon,

The army of the devil shall tremble.
For their fate they will weep.
And the righteous shall rejoice
As their deliverance draws nigh.

Then in that hour I shall be comforted.
My burden of sin licked up by the flames.
No longer my eyes to behold sorrow,
Or my ears endure the rude jest of a maddened
throng.
Hunger, pain, poverty, all buried in the ashes.
Greed, illness, the grave wiped out in the cleansing
flames.

How I long for that hour!
How my heart desires to see the end of sin!
May my prayer ever be for Thy soon return!
May my heart despise the burden of sin,
And seek comfort only in living for Thee!

My Eyes are Tired of This Earth!

Tired eyes,
Tired dreams,
Reruns of memories long ago,
Silly hopes,
Foolish dreams,
Secret longings waiting to be free.

Filled with wonder,
Filled with unspoken awe,
Trying to trust in the Divine hand.

Needing patience,
Needing prayer,
Trying to learn to lean on the Almighty's arm.

Longing for love so pure and free,
Knowing on earth it shall never be.
Waiting for Heaven to set me free.

And break free of the shell of sin and sorrow,
At last to grow in beauty and grace.

Someday those tired eyes will be free.
The longing of my heart to at last be fulfilled.
At last in that land of Heavenly glory to be satisfied,
Knowing through all my lonely days that my Savior
has never strayed.
Seeing how my lonely heart was led through the Red
Sea waters,
But only for my greater good.

The questions born of a thousand sorrows,
At last to be answered.
The memories of a million painful hours to be
erased,
Surrounded by Heaven's blinding, unsurpassable,
and indescribable glory.
There I will at last,
Once and forever more say that;
My heart is at rest.
My world is at peace.
Nothing can or ever will disturb the precious joy that
has filled my heart to overflowing,
For pain and suffering are no more!

Lost in endless joy,
Shedding my tarnished remnant layers of skin I will
ever grow to reflect the perfect matchless love of the
King of Kings.
My love and appreciation for the wondrous sacrifice,

So hard to comprehend,
Will only be magnified through the ceaseless passing
ages.
My songs of grace will only grow sweeter and more
certain as I study from His unceasing fountain of
wonders.

There all of my fondest hopes will come alive.
My mind and body enjoy a perfect union.
And by the Savior's side I shall have nothing to
make me feel shame.
My ugliness He will turn to beauty.
My frailty He will turn to healthy joy.

Oh for that day!
Oh for that unknown hour!
When at last I shall see that cloud,
When at last I am headed home,
And with my tired eyes I will tread into partake of
Heaven's unspeakable joy!

He is Coming

He is coming around the corner.
He is coming in the clouds.
He is coming with a retinue of angels.
He is coming with the shout of victory.
He is coming with trumpet of rejoicing.
He is coming with the sword of power.
He is coming as a conqueror.
He is coming to bring an end to sin and sorrow.
He is coming to bring His people home.
He is coming at the midnight hour.
He is coming to take me home.

If Only the King Would Return!

How hard it is to wait for the king's return as the world around begins to crumble.
Violence grows stronger with each passing day.
Love dies as hate springs into every heart and souls of man.
Even the sacred sanctuary has become the nesting place for the hungering, prancing, nervously pacing wolves and hawks.

Viperous instincts have defaced the image of peace.
Songs of war have replaced the tenderly calling pipes of peace.
Nations are growing angrier as the angel of strife flutters his fearful, dreadful, deadly wings among the unprepared shelter less corners of the earth.
No home is safe,
No building is secure,

No towering mountain lofty enough,
No coweringly hole sufficiently low,
No bottomless cavernous pit endless enough,
No watery hideaway locked far enough within the oven warm bowels of the earth,
To secure from the wrath of the lion seeking to devour and destroy poor defenseless humanity,
To hide from the battle that is yet to come,
Or to hide from the eyes of the one that is ever seeking to save and rescue the weary and the battle scarred lost.

Even the wind and the waves grow restless for deliverance.
Slipping from their bounds time after time they destroy the proud works of the selfish mighty.
Earthquakes and tornados level buildings meant to challenge the power of the gracious saving King.
All nature struggles with the growing burden of the defiant inhabitants.
Struggling to bear each weight they place upon their strained and helpless shoulders.

As I see the world crumbling around me I ask now how long dear Lord before you silence the fearful voice of strife and answer the mocking insults of the defiant ones?
How long before you come and put an end to the intensifying pangs of sin?
The earth runs red with the blood of the innocent ones slain for the selfish gains of a few.

The wrath of the devil knows no boundary,
While the insanity of man finds no end to its pitiful
depths.

Ruler and commoner sin together.
Each vying for the opportunity to out sin the other,
Their depravity seems to have no limits as they build
a pit to roast the weak,
To destroy the helpless,
To hurl down the innocent little tender suffering
lambs.

Rise up o Lord and cleanse Your sanctuary!
Rise up and cleanse away the vileness from my sin
filled heart!
Do not start with the mocking world!
But prepare my heart for the final hour.
Remove all taints of ugliness that defile and stain,
Wash away any defiling smudges of evil,
And grant me a heart prepared to receive the Latter
Rain.

Come soon dear Lord!
Lest all goodness be destroyed from off of the face
of the earth.
Lest the redeemed grow tired of watching and
waiting,
And sadly fall into the deadly, toxic,
And suffocating trap of sin.

Our bodies growing numb from the cold,

Our home hungering hearts
Shirk from the ghastly and oh so grizzly sights,
And our aching souls
Have been worn down by the horrifying sounds of
the unfettered sin that parades all around us.
The arrows of the wicked are being sharpened as
they prepare for the battle of the final hour,
And sadly we are growing so warm and sleepy,
So comfortable and tame,
And do not see the flares of danger lighting up all
around us.

Come and put an end to the misery.
Do away with sin forever.
Rescue the redeemed from the hands of the enemy.
And make this earth new in Your infinite purity,
At last to reflect
Your infinite all-knowing wisdom,
And to once more be a glowing bastion of Your
infinite unyielding love.

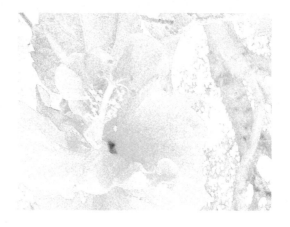

The King Draws Near

Flowers bloom at a whisper.
Mountains rise at a thought.
One command brings forth a universe.

With the wave of a hand oceans begin to flow.
A turn of the head brings a grass covered valley into place
In the twinkle of an eye bright stars fill the night sky.

Rivers flow at a wish.
Birds appear at a heartbeat.
Gentle breezes blow at the turn of a head.

Songs of glory rise from grateful throats.
Words of hope lie on all tongues.
Thoughts of worship fill perfect minds.

For the Maker of the Universe draws near,
His power is like no other.

His tender voice made of music.

The flowers of the valley bend in reverence.
The wind stops at his approach.
The earth below His holy feet trembles softly.

Rows of perfect beings fold their hands solemnly.
Anxiously they wait to hear Him speak.
The joy within their hearts overflowing and
reflecting upon their glorious faces.

No joy could be more precious.
No dream could be more glorious.
For the King of Kings now stands in their humble
midst.

THE MAKER OF THE UNIVERSE DRAWS NEAR

Flowers bloom a whisper.
Mountains rise at a thought.
One command brings forth a universe.

With the wave of a hand oceans began to flow.
A turn of the head brings a grass-covered valley into place
In the twinkle of an eye stars fill the night sky.

Rivers flow at a wish.
Birds appear at a heartbeat.
Gentle breezes blow at the turn of a head.
Words of hope lie on all tongues.
Thoughts of worship fill perfect minds.

For the Maker of the Universe draws near.

His powers like no other.
His tender voice made of music.

The flowers of the valley bend in reverence.
The wind stops as his approach.
The earth below His holy feet trembles softly.
Rows of perfect beings fold their hands solemnly.
Anxiously they wait to hear Him speak.
The joy in their hearts reflecting on their faces.

No joy could be more precious.
No dream could be more glorious.
For the King of Kings stand in their midst.

When You Come

When you come dear LORD,
What will it be like?
Will the earth reel like a drunkard under the feet of
the Redeemer?
Will the sear rise high in the sight of Thy purchase?
Will the worthies tried by hottest fire feel the
elements break for in final war as they self-destruct
before Thy cleansing presence?
What will Thy people feel as Thy cloud sprouts forth
like a mighty tree?

When you come dear LORD,
Who will stand?
Will I be afraid to meet your penetrating gaze?
Will my heart melt in fear under Your holy
inspection?
Will I be ready to welcome You as the earth melts
with fervent heat?

How will my human heart endure the piercing moans of the lost as they succumb to the running power of Thy all-consuming glory?

What will it truly be like at that final ultimate fearful thundering earth quaking hour of Thy coming when forever I must stand before Thee like I am?
When as sinner or washed in the blood my book is sealed,
My decision is ultimately made.
One way or the other,
I must stand.
Clean or unclean,
Pure or impure,
I must eternally remain.

How will it feel on that fearful earth staggering day when the elements rain down in unspeakable terror?
When the fires of the deep break forth,
When the fountains of the earth spit forth their unseen reserves.

Will my heart be ready?
Will my heart be pure?
Will I have made the right choice?
Or will I have wandered and squandered away my final fleeting hours in search of trivial nothings?
Throwing away eternal bliss and purity for rusted nails that have been beaten out to look like gold?
Will it be shown that for a few dingy motheaten rags, I have exchanged the beauty of heaven?

Or sold my eternal home,
For a plate of cold beans?

Oh dear LORD,
What will that long looked forward day be like?
What will that day of glory and hope be,
If for the chance to enjoy a few ephemeral pleasures
I am not ready?
Will that day,
Overflowing with promise,
Prove to be a day of breathless joy,
Or will it be the a day of passionate sorrow,
As I mourn for what might have been,
What would have been if I had only given the King
my heart?

Either it will be the beginning of hope or the ending
of peace.
Either it will be the culmination of all my hopes,
The starting point of all my dreams,
As I freely drink of fountain of life,
Or it will be the crashing end
Of all my hope and dreams.
As a sea of tears I shed,
For the home of peace,
The land of overflowing goodness,
That I shall never see.

What a day!
What strange event that will be.
How hard it is to imagine.

How hard it is to picture in all its untapped wonder
and life changing glory.

Looked forward to by some,
Dreaded by others,
Scoffed at by many,
Looked on narrowly by those who view it to be just
an old fabled wives tale,
Much of its beauty and color has been lost and
tarnished.
Much of its charm has faded into the background.

Lost through fear,
Lost through ignorance,
Lost somewhere under a hectic daze,
And buried under a mountain of skepticism,
So much of its power,
Its precious bounty has been frittered away.
Until it seems like a merry fable,
A charming story of what might be,
Of what could be if mankind would mend their
ways.

Oh what will it be like when You come?
What will it really be like on that great and dreadful
day?
When that final hour tolls will I be ready?
Will my heart have passed the test?
Will I long to meet Your steady firm gaze?
Will I want to see that breathless day?

I may not know the half of what that hour will be like.
No poet's pen,
No artist brush,
No orator can even hope to begin to describe that solemn scene,
When man stands for the first time face to face before His God,
When for the first time since Jesus walked this earth two thousand years ago,
Man looks into the face of the Kings of Kings.
No human word can possibly describe,
No melody is strong enough to express the deep feelings of wonder and fear
When man faces His God,
When he stands before the All-mighty Judge,
And discovers too late that though God is love,
Out of love for those who cling to their sins,
That they will perish with the sins to which their hands stubbornly cling.
That justice demands that with the sins they have firmly wrapped their arms around,
And like a rebellious tantrum throwing child,
Cling too with all their might,
They must now perish.
For as long as their arms, hearts, wills, and lives are interlaced with sin,
As long as their souls are so willfully and firmly entwined with iniquity,
As long as sin and person remain willfully and stubbornly one and the same,

What choice does He have but to kindly release the
universe from the bondage of sin?
And how can He put away the sin,
How can He erase the curse,
without damaging the sinner
if with iron grasp man does stubbornly cling to it?

Oh what a day,
What a strange day it will be.
Yet what a wonderful day when Satan is at last put in
chains,
When his power to tempt and destroy are no more.
When for a thousand years,
During his trial by the righteous of earth,
Awaiting his final day of reckoning,
Awaiting his fearful day of sentencing,
He is forced to wander the empty caverns of earth.
When for centuries stowed up by active labor,
Hunting and destroying the lives of man,
He is left to sit in earth's empty cell,
There to consider his scandalous ways,
And to ponder his disreputable course.

Oh how the universe will sing!
Oh how the angels will glorify Thy holy of holiest
names!
How the redeemed will drop before Thy feet and
honor You for endless ages to come.

What a strange and fearful day it will be when you
come.

Filled with unusual sights and sounds,
Filled with fear and wondering,
Filled with hope and prayer,
And filled with promise and beauty.

It is a time of soul searching for all,
It is a time of great earnest joy for all.
It is a day of fear to those who do not know and
recognize God's name,
But for the people of God it will be the sweetest
symphony of promise.
It will be the beginning of every happiness,
The begging of life unlimited,
Of life unfettered by time,
Unfettered by sickness,
And unfettered by space and immobility.

It will be the beginning of a new world of limitless
possibilities where one can travel to the moon,
Become an artist,
Be a musician,
Write a symphony,
Work with lions,
Climb a mountain,
Scuba dive,
Garden,
Cook,
Study math and science,
Be a history buff,
Be a poet,
Build a castle,

Travel to worlds yet unknown,
And still have a long list of interest pursuits
Just waiting to be explored and time enough left to
explore each and every one to one's heart's content.

This is the glory and wonder of that day.
This is the beauty of that so longed for hour.
How I hope that You come soon Dear Lord.
How I hope that You do not linger.
How I hope and pray that my heart is right with you.
How I hope and pray that your heart is right too.

For the invitation is yours as well as mine.
Jesus asks us one and all.
His door is open to all.
He invites everyone to freely come.
There is no sinner that has sinned to great,
There is no nation that is too high or too poor.
There is no door that is too small or too mighty.
There is no nationality that He does not know.
There is no type that He will not reach.

My Jesus loves every man and every woman.
He came to seek and to save the lost.
He died for every man, woman, and child,
Even those who turn and walk away.
He spilt His blood so all can one day choose to be
free.
He spilt His blood so all can choose to live or die.

This is the beauty of that final hour.

It need not be fierce and trembling.
It might have been mighty
But it need not have been tempestuous,
But only full of the greatest rejoicing.

Yet it need not be a day of sadness for your heart.
It need not be a day of fear and trembling for your
soul.
Why not enter the ark prepared for the great and
solemn day.
Wash yourself in the blood of the lamb and be clean.
Wash your heart,
Ask and receive the free gift of salvation.

Make your life new by giving it to Jesus.
Make your life new in Him who gave His all.
And you will see that He has a better way.
That what little you lose is worth more than all the
gold and silver of the universe.
That the wages of sin is death,
But the gift of God truly is life eternal!

CHAPTER 8
POETRY OF VICTORY

Viva Eternidad!

Viva Eternidad
Quiries viva eternidad?
Christo es vivir eternidad.

Do you want to live a full life?
Do you crave abundant joy?
Do you desire hope that never fails?
Do you long for peace of heart more than phantom
riches?

Do you dream of doing something worthy of
remembrance by endless generations?
Do you wish to drink from a fountain of life that has
no end?

If this is your desire,
If this is your dream,
There is only one choice,
There is only one answer.

In Jesus only will you find the well of happiness.
In Jesus alone will you be able to ride the swelling
waves of uncertainty.
In Jesus you will find the key to unlock the door of
eternal life.
In Jesus your greatest wishes will be answered.

For Jesus is the only source of peace,
HE is the fountain of LIFE,
FULL,
OVERFLOWING,
AND EVERLASTING!

For Jesus is Vivir Eternidad!

The Hour is Here

The hour is near
The hour is here
Like an overflowing river
Shall flood our hearts

Like nourishing drops of dew to a wilting land
Thy Guiding Spirit shall freely be bestowed
Opening the eyes of the blind
And enlightening the understanding of fools

Oh how great will be Thy glory!
Oh how great will be our need!
As midnight's frightful hour nears
World and spirits unite
To proclaim their seeming victory

When unseen hands guide the world
Leading old and young
Rich and poor

Wise and foolish
To proclaim a feast of jubilee

Shouting and writhing
Feasting and dancing
Their merry song of triumph will ascend
In the hour of their greatest joy
When confident that Your Spirit they have destroyed
Your glory like a flaming sword shall pierce the darkness.
Revealing the secrets of men's perverse heart,
And showing all the only true path to eternal life.

Victory

Victory
Is mine to shout.
With great joy I march past Heaven's glorious arch.
With palm branch waving
Keeping time to the ecstatic song of my heart
As sin
A distant memory
Fades further and further from my mind.
To become a speck,
An infinitesimal shadow,
In my awestruck memory banks.
That now overflow in amazement
At Heaven's unimaginable glory.
With tingling fingers
I lift my hand
To strike the melodious chord.
To declare to all
My hearts wonder
To know once and forever
That I am free to march the streets of glory!

Forever
Acrostic #1

Forever
Oh what a thought that
Races through my head
Everlasting life
Vital promise
Ecstatic joy
Rejuvenates my heart and fills my life with joy

Victory
Acrostic 1

Victory
Is receiving a new name in
Christ
To be born again and obtain the reward of the
Overcomer and to
Reap the recompense of the faithful in the
Year of our Lord

Poems of Faith

ABOUT THE AUTHOR

Katherine B. Parilli stumbled upon her love of writing thanks in great part to her father who homeschooled her in the second and seventh grade. Blessed with a love of reading, but seemingly possessing no talent for writing, Katherine would virtually rewrite the book for her book report. Her Father, not content to have her rewrite the book for her reports, he insisted that she write, rewrite, and rewrite again and again until nearly in tears, she was finally able to write a few semi thoughtful sentences.

Still it was not until her first year of high school when this rigorous training suddenly blossomed into a love of writing everything from poetry and short stories, to novels and short research articles.

Poetry From the Heart: Poems of Faith is her first book to be published. But she is already in the process of writing her second book of poetry as well as collection of short stories. She occasionally contributes some of her poems to the Make Time for Happy 101 blog and You Tube sites and also has her own You Tube Channel called Poetry From the Heart as well as writes a blog called Reflections about Life

Printed in Great Britain
by Amazon

74652851R00068